The
CTO ¦ CIO
Bible

The Mission, Objectives,
Strategies and Tactics

Needed to Be A
Super Successful
CTO ¦ CIO

RORIE DEVINE

This book is dedicated to my darling wife and family (for putting up with me waking up in the middle of the night to use my laptop) and to my oldest friend Ian...not that he will ever read it having said it "sounds well dull".

☞, Ó and ! highlight key points.

« marks insight directly from my network.

Ð is a book definitely worth reading.

‡ are stories from the ups and downs of my career.

Note: I'm going to use SHe rather than He/She as the non-gender specific pronoun in this book by the way...sorry if it annoys anyone but I think it looks less clunky.

TABLE OF CONTENTS

OUR MISSION

In this CTO ¦ CIO Bible I'll talk about using a Mission, Objectives Strategies and Tactics approach to being a super successful CTO ¦ CIO. Our MISSION in this CTO ¦ CIO Bible is therefore...

TO MAKE OUR COMPANIES
SUPER SUCCESSFUL
BY BEING A
SUPER SUCCESSFUL
CTO ¦ CIO

Great, now we have our MISSION what are the best OBJECTIVES, STRATEGIES and TACTICS to achieve it?!?

☞ CEO's love seeing a MOST because they *really* like the concept of making both big picture strategic progress as well as moving the business forward with impactful near term delivery ...

« The most important thing about being a Tech Leader is making sure you empower your people, set them up for success and hold them accountable for the results.
                    Emanuele Blanco CTO Moneyfarm

! Focus your efforts where it will affect your customers...try to innovate at the customer touch points (web sites, apps etc.) not way down the stack where your efforts will have little/no effect on customer satisfaction.

MOST

What everyone needs these days is a strategic framework that informs and embraces change and actually makes tactical execution *more* effective.

MISSION
WHY we want/need to make the journey

OBJECTIVES
WHAT we want to achieve

STRATEGIES
HOW we will achieve our Objectives

TACTICS
The 5-10 things we will DO now

The Strategies are a **How** not a **What** and they can and *should* change any time something material changes in their context.

☛ Don't choose more than 5-10 tactics per quarter to deliver your Strategies...any more than that makes the implicit "prioritisation" pointless...pick a mix of safe/straightforward/stretch goals ... it's always important to get some wins on the board...

! The US Navy talks about a "ship, shipmate, self" hierarchy when looking at the impact and scope of decision making. Huge business impact can be achieved by identifying and successfully implementing a series of low effort-high impact initiatives.

Alastair Campbell talked about objectives, strategy and tactics in his excellent book "Winners: And How They Succeed" (available at https://amzn.to/3635QaD). In 2017 I augmented it with a Mission to create the MOST Framework...

Objectives

Ð "Good to Great: Why Some Companies Make the Leap...and Others Don't" by James C. Collins is a fascinating analysis of what the companies that step up to greatness have in common. One of the key lessons is ""First Who, then What?" or in other words get the right people on the bus...available at https://amzn.to/2EUGmQS

« The most important thing about being a Tech leader is not the technology. It's building teams of diverse talent, giving them a purpose they can be passionate about and empowering them to deliver - while guiding and supporting them to fulfil their potential to the benefit of the business.

Rich Phillips Consultant CTO Cinteq

So what Objectives should a successful CTO ¦ CIO set, and what are the most important things to focus on?

Urgency

! If you think about all of the great people you've worked with in the past some of the things that they probably have in common are that they are **passionate** about what they do, they have **energy** and they bring u**rgency**.

☛ All great leaders bring urgency into everything they do. They don't set people up for failure (all of their goals are ambitious but achievable) but they want the benefits from the initiative *so* much that they can't wait to get it and want it *now*.

Malcolm Gladwell thinks that Steve Jobs didn't achieve what he achieved because of intellect or hard work but because of his urgency. "Urgency," Gladwell declared, "characterizes Jobs and other immortal entrepreneurs. Jobs is rushed — he's urgent — and that was a part of his genius." The difference isn't resources," Gladwell said. "It's attitude."

‡ One of the start-up CEO's I worked for used to come into work every Monday and manufacture a sense of crisis and high urgency around a carefully chosen single problem or opportunity. We'd all focus to make progress on the issue before Monday when we knew the cycle would start all over again. By "stirring the pot" like this the CEO ensured the team were always moving forward with high focus and urgency.

« The most important thing about being a Tech Leader is admitting when you get something wrong and changing course to correct. Teams will quickly lose patience with and faith in leaders who can't say those simple words.

Ollie Cook, Staff SRE, Google

! **BUSYNESS IS BAD FOR BUSINESS** ... don't make the mistake of confusing busyness with urgency. Urgency is an impatience to *achieve* business outcomes...it is not the same thing as being busy with activities that may or may not lead to positive business outcomes.

Clarity

! In my experience there are two kinds of people... people who like to make things simpler and clearer and people who get some sort of perverse pleasure dealing with complexity and therefore feel no need to clarify things or situations.

Don't be lazy...always make the effort to clarify and simplify situations or problems. Making a concept or message clearer makes it easier to communicate and massively increases its chances of landing successfully...

« The most important thing about being a technology leader is recognising that you are always learning and always needing to reinvent yourself. We are fortunate in our roles that the continuous evolution of technology along with the changes in working practises and people's needs brings with it excitement and a challenge.

Alex Farr CIO Strictly Education Ltd

! A quote attributed to Blaise Pascal is "I have made this longer than usual because I have not had time to make it shorter"....as leaders we *always* need to make it shorter...

Đ "How to Build a Billion Dollar App: Discover the Secrets of the Most Successful Entrepreneurs of Our Time" by George Berkowski is a very insightful and comprehensive description of how to build and launch successful apps...and I'm saying that even though I'm featured in it as "Rory" Devine...thanks George...available at https://amzn.to/362rEmF

! As they mature as a leader a lot of people go through a stage where they focus on what is best for their team rather than their company. Maybe it's a natural stage of the leadership journey but it's essential that at the C level we all see our jobs as co-delivering the company business plan.

Delivery

Delivery is one of those concepts that is hard to pin down objectively because it is the aggregate of a lot of attitudes, behaviours and impact measures.

Every CEO knows when they're not getting as much delivery as they would like and they're not usually shy in voicing their opinion...I like to create a small full stack "Rapid Development" team responsible for weekly drops of tactical fixes and enhancements. Never let the quick and easy stuff get stuck behind the big and hard stuff....

! When asked by a stakeholder as to whether something can be done don't suck through your teeth but always respond along the lines of "let's look at it, if it's possible we'll do it..." Your stakeholders need to trust that you genuinely *want* to get their things done. Once people trust that you would deliver to their dates if it was possible then they will believe you if you say it isn't possible...

✝ I quite often spend at least some time in my interim engagements debating development metrics with the CEO. The CEO thinks they're not getting enough delivery and they hope they might be able to prove it using scrum story points per sprint or whatever.

The disappointing truth is that due to the wide variety in how story points are measured and used by each individual team these sort of metrics are only really useful for tracking the trajectory and progress of individual teams. Story points are pretty meaningless when comparing across teams. Some CEOs eventually see that and others never really lose their suspicion that there is a conspiracy to help teams avoid objective scrutiny.

« The most interesting thing about being a Tech Leader is there has never been a better time to deliver real and rapid business change through the delivery of innovative technology that really works. That is what every CIO should strive for given the tools available in a digital world.

Ian Woosey CIO Clarion Housing Group

Agility

The Manifesto for Agile Software Development (agilemanifesto.org) was created in 2001 with four key principles saying that we should value...

> Individuals and interactions over processes and tools.
> Working software over comprehensive documentation.
> Customer collaboration over contract negotiation.
> Responding to change over following a plan.

Ó Agile is a How not a What. There are no prizes for the purest and most orthodox implementation of Agile. If a team isn't focussing on creating working software then it might have fallen into the trap of admiring the process rather than delivering business impact.

☞ Introducing Agile is one of the few truly transformative things you can do for a business. Use Retrospective sessions to make sure your approach is adaptive and is always improving...

☛ "Agile" principles can also be used very effectively to deliver growth rather than software (see **Appendix 05**)

Ó Agile doesn't mean "no deadlines", "no documentation", "no interference" or any of the other excuses Agile zealots use to avoid doing the things they don't want to do. Alarm bells should ring loudly if you hear the words "pair programming". Whether you like it or not you may have joined the congregation at a high church of Agile...

‡ There is an allegory used in Agile circles about a chicken and a pig to point out the difference between commitment and involvement during daily stand-ups. One day the chicken decides that the two should start a restaurant. "What should we call it?" says the pig. The chicken thinks and suggests, "Ham and Eggs!" To which the pig replies, "No thanks, I'd be committed. You'd only be involved".

Simplicity

Alongside the benefits of a focus on clarity there are massive benefits to be obtained from driving simplicity in everything you do. Businesses can end up with horrendously complicated technology and process landscapes if they don't actively manage their technology architecture and operating model complexity.

Ó People are happy to build and launch things but it is very rare to see an initiative removing software, systems or processes. A notable exception was a Fintech I worked at where the legacy Ruby monolith was given a name ("Frankie" as in Frankenstein) and a LOC (Lines Of Code) reduction OKR was selected by one of the teams.

☞ Sponsor initiatives to simplify your technology estate and operating model. It's not as glamorous as launching a new product ¦ service but you will definitely make things quicker | cheaper.

☛ Supplier rationalisation is an often overlooked way of simplifying and taking cost out of your business. You won't win many fans at the suppliers you rationalise but the benefits can be significant.

‡ I was at a media business that was being disrupted by "digital" products and services. The Head Of Operations came to me to tell me that when customers bought our new package of our services they were getting up to fifteen confirmation letters through the post. Although it wasn't my direct area of responsibility I launched a project with the simple, clear and unambiguous scope of "Stop the envelopes".

Once launched my most important contribution to the project was to say "No – just stop the envelopes" every time a team tried to derail or delay the project by saying they needed a new tool, team, process or whatever. The project completely nailed its goal...it was calculated at the time that 1.5 million envelopes per year were stopped from being sent and the customer satisfaction, cost and environmental benefits were huge.

Accountability

One of the things that marks out a high performer is their desire to seek out and take accountability for business outcomes. You can't *take* accountability as a CTO | CIO if you can't *give* it as well.

There are no silver bullets in changing a team's performance but if there were silver bullets introducing a culture of accountability would be one of them. I like to separate "Build" and "Run" when setting teams up otherwise the accountability for software or service delivery is massively diluted both ways.

Ó When introducing a culture of accountability some people will confuse it with a blame culture. Explain to them that we want to increase ownership of business outcomes not find people to blame when things go wrong.

Ó Don't create any structures that set up responsibility without control (such as making someone accountable for the performance of an external supplier, or separate team). That is a great way to set people up for failure.

Đ "Will it Make the Boat Go Faster? Olympic-winning Strategies for Everyday Success" by Harriet Beveridge and Ben Hunt-Davis is a brilliant book by a rowing Olympic gold medallist and an executive coach showing how the strategies Ben used to win an Olympic gold medal can be applied to a lot of areas in business and life generally...available at https://amzn.to/2ZuznHL

Ó The response to constructive feedback when telling someone there are performance issues is telling. A performer will ask for more feedback and help turning the situation around but an under performer will say that the feedback has negatively affected their morale.

STRATEGIES

Ó Strategies need to be living, breathing things. They are not fixed plans carved in stone and only dusted off occasionally. Out of date strategies are useless strategies.

☞ You may need to deploy a dual track or bi-modal strategy to achieve all of your objectives. One side of your strategy could be to pay back technical debt in parallel with the other side of the strategy innovating via a "game changer".

☞ The IT strategy needs to be presented alongside the business strategy. The IT strategy both informs, and is informed by, the business strategy.

Success via Technology

Ó Some people would argue that the primary role of a CTO ¦ CIO is to use technology to make their company successful. I think there is a lot of truth in that but let's not forget that all leaders execute through people not technology at the end of the day.

☛ A focus on business success is crucial...a theme running through this book is that great CTO ¦ CIO's focus relentlessly on business value and outcomes in anything and everything they do.

Ó Some CTO ¦ CIO's make the mistake of focusing on input or internal metrics (such as deployment frequency, code quality etc.) rather than the thing that really matters...namely revenue, profit, costs or whatever...

Ó Be very, very careful what behaviours you encourage when choosing metrics. I'm convinced that we get so many emails from LinkedIn because since Microsoft's acquisition of LinkedIn the CEO of Microsoft, Satya Nadell, and his C-suite have a compensation scheme partly based on the "number of times logged-in members visit LinkedIn, separated by 30 minutes of inactivity".

☛ Of course a technologist's primary tool box is technology (rather than marketing or whatever) so it is *always* part of a CTO ¦ CIO's job to use technology to make things quicker, better or cheaper for their company.

Ð "Freakonomics: A Rogue Economist Explores the Hidden Side of Everything" by Steven D. Levitt and Stephen J. Dubner is a fascinating look at the difference between causation and connectivity and why drug dealers live with their mothers...available **at** https://amzn.to/2Q2VTVi

Competitive Advantage

❚ The most effective way to make your business successful is to give it a competitive advantage. If a business has competitive advantage then it can do things other businesses can't do, or it can do the things other businesses do quicker, better or cheaper.

Ó To create competitive advantage you and your team need to do something better than *all* of the competitor's teams in your industry. Creating competitive advantage is therefore easy to say but not easy to do.

‡ When I was at Betfair we were matching online transactions at such low latency (5-10 milliseconds) that a delegation from the London Stock Exchange visited us to ask us how we were doing it...

☛ One route to competitive advantage is with actionable insight from Data. I have embedded a Data Scientist within all of the scrum teams at a number of companies. At Hailo the "Driver" Team found a number of creative ways to increase the Driver Acceptance Rate by deriving actionable insight from data.

« The most important thing about being a Tech Leader is to ensure that you make room for innovation. Create a space that allows people to innovate and try new ideas and deliver organisational value rapidly in an iterative manner.

Dave Roberts CIO Radius Payment Solutions

Ð "High output management" by Andrew Grove is full of great advice from the former CEO of Intel about how to build and run a company as a set of repeatable production processes. As Andy puts it "manage short-term objectives based on long-term plans"... sound familiar? Available at https://amzn.to/2QiG9Mw

What & How

Ó Don't make the mistake of treating a How as a What. Which language you write your software in is a How. Your web site visitor to user conversion rate is a What.

☞ Spend as much time as possible working on the What not the How. Try to do things that directly affect the What rather than the How which at best will have a second order effect on the What.

Ó When choosing your When always try to deliver a Minimum Viable Product early, and then test and learn. Avoid "drive by MVPs" whereby a sub-standard version of the product is launched by a team that quickly moves on to the next thing without iterating and improving it. Aim for what some people are calling a Minimum Lovable Product.

Ó Writing a functional specification takes too long, always contains omissions and errors, and by the time the functionality is delivered the real world will have moved on so the what the customer wants ¦ needs will have changed.

☞ It is much better to pilot ¦ prototype and then iterate based on direct customer usage than to try to predict and plan the future based on imperfect data in a changing world...

☞ An alternative to classic two week sprint Scrum agile is to use a more "Kanban" rhythm where time-boxed development is dropped, estimation is optional or out completely and velocity metrics are replaced by cycle time.

Manage Relationships

A massive part of the CTO ¦ CIO role is managing the IT Team's reputation and relationship with all of the key stakeholders in the business. The relationships with the other C Suite people are probably the most important relationships that a CTO ¦ CIO has to manage.

‡ I found my first executive committee meeting at a very traditional FTSE 200 business very intimidating. Everyone sat "suited and booted" in the oak panelled boardroom listening to the CEO monologue as a tea lady served tea in a bone china tea set. I'm not sure that I contributed much and as I was leaving the CEO took me aside and said "Rorie, you are paid to talk". I made sure they had to stop me talking in subsequent meetings...

☞ By a country mile the most important relationship a CTO ¦ CIO has to manage is with his ¦ her line manager, which is normally the CEO. It's critical that the CTO | CIO is seen to understand, support and deliver on the CEO's agenda.

Ó A lot of IT teams fall into the trap of setting up Adult-Child relationships with their colleagues by mandating what they can and can't do and chastising them if they break the "rules". Adult-Adult relationships with your colleagues are much more effective...there is no need to patronise them.

! The CTO ¦ CIO has the most to lose if the relationship with their boss breaks down so it is *very* much the CTO ¦ CIO's job to proactively manage this relationship. The CEO doesn't have time to think "what good work did the CTO ¦ CIO do this week?" so make it easy for the CEO by telling them at least once a week about all the good work you and your team are doing.

☛ A lot of CTO ¦ CIO's aren't comfortable "blowing their own trumpet" so celebrate the successes of your team and the people in it rather than yourself. You're accountable and responsible for the team's performance so it's the same thing at the end of the day. Copying the CEO in a "Rorie's Ramblings" like email is a great way of achieving this.

Product

Ó Whether we like it or not the two sides of the product development coin are normally the Product and Tech teams. They need to work very closely together if competitive advantage is going to be created for the company.

! Great Product Owners | Managers protect their development teams from unproductive work. Any time developers aren't creating code is sub optimal...minimise the amount of time developers spend in meetings.

☞ I have a lot of empathy for a Chief Product Officer in a founder driven company...if they agree with everything the founder says then they will eventually get fired for "not adding any value" but if they clash with the founder too often then they will eventually get fired for "not sharing the vision"... CPO's are only choosing how to fail in some situations ...

Ó It is normally a bit of a loveless marriage between Product and Tech but a CTO | CIO needs to support and make their CPO successful. The company won't be successful if the Product team aren't leading the charge on the product-market fit.

☨ I've worked with some great and some awful CPOs over the years. A great CPO (like Jonathon Moore currently a Partner at Silicon Valley Product Group) understands that great Product Owners ¦ Managers credit their engineers when things go well and take the blame when things don't go so well. Bad Product Owners ¦ Managers do the opposite...

Đ "Who Moved My Cheese: An Amazing Way to Deal with Change in Your Work and in Your Life" by Dr Spencer Johnson uses two mice and two human characters (yes really) to consider change and how to deal with it. Well worth a read and it has sold 25 million copies worldwide apparently...available at https://amzn.to/37iVxj7. Two animal characters will shamelessly be introduced into the second edition of this book if sales don't go very well...

People Game Changers

Outsourcing - if your company has huge over capacity or under performing teams then a win/win relationship with a genuinely good outsourced provider might change the game for your company.

! You are dancing with the devil when you sign an outsourcing deal. You will probably be dealing with a huge supplier legal team very experienced in creating long win/lose contracts. Even if the upfront costs look attractive be careful of the cost of change in your outsourcing contact.

Insourcing - if your company has win/lose relationships with ineffective or expensive suppliers then insourcing the work might change the game for your company. Increased business impact for 50% of the costs is possible when fixing bad outsourcing relationships.

Process Game Changers

☞ Leveraging a modern SaaS platform (such as Salesforce) can change the game for some businesses. Avoid customising these platforms though, configure don't code...

☞ Simplifying via supplier rationalisation is a great way to take cost and complexity out of your business. Are all of your suppliers *really* essential? Sunsetting a supplier will take cost and a lot of integration and reconciliation complexity away.

Ó You are dancing with the devil again when you implement an ERP system. If you standardise your business processes to match the software (rather than the other way around) and avoid custom point to point interfaces to other systems like the plague then the ERP system *may* not ultimately be an expensive and inflexible constraint on your business.

Tech Game Changers

☛The Cloud genuinely changes the game in IT by providing variable cost and variable capacity infrastructure available behind powerful management software. AWS (Amazon Web Services) and GCP (Google Cloud Platform) are also doing a great job of democratising access to technologies such as machine learning and image recognition.

People lacking Cloud skills used to quote "Security" as an excuse not to move to The Cloud but it is now possible to encrypt your data both in transit and at rest in AWS and GCP. Encryption makes your data an order of magnitude more secure than it would be in the average corporate data centre.

☛It's very easy to waste a lot of money with cloud providers. Make sure your team carefully controls environment creation and stands down environments when they're not being used.

APIs

☞ Creating a public Application Programming Interface enables businesses to take their product | service to new markets/customers and increase the value of their product | service by integrating third party data or functionality.

! The write once/use many times nature of an API allows companies to leverage their IT investment by 10's or even 100's of times.

‡ Success was not guaranteed during the early years at Betfair and I'm convinced that the creation of a public API was one of the main reasons it beat the imitators and competition. (It eventually IPO'd on the London Stock Exchange for £1.5/$2.0 Billion). Moneyfarm has just announced the largest API-based digital wealth management partnership in Europe.

PWAs

☞ Creating a single Progressive Web App will allow you to deliver web and native iOS | Android app like experiences from one single integrated platform. That could deliver a 66% cost saving or a 300% increase in development velocity.

Ó Apple's Safari implementation of PWA isn't as good as Google's Chrome implementation but there aren't any issues that can't be fixed with a bit of JavaScript.

☞ Turning a web page into a PWA isn't as hard as you might think...all you need to do is create a JSON manifest file (showing where the static assets are) the serviceworker JavaScript and put a couple of tags in the HTML pointing to them...ta da!

Google Go/golang

In golang Google created a back end platform services language that is easier to learn, easier to code, easier to deploy, faster and more cost-effective than all of the alternatives. **See** Appendix 04 **for more detail**...

At Hailo we re-platformed from PHP/Java to a golang micro-services platform and saw a 60% reduction in AWS cost per transaction as we scaled up past 1,000,000 users...

The most important thing about being a Tech Leader is to set a path, empower your team then communicate, communicate, communicate, listen, listen, listen. Be clear and be curious.

Steve Homan CTO Metapack

TACTICS

To implement your strategies you need to carefully choose 5-10 (and *only* 5-10) tactics per quarter. Make sure your tactics are self-describing things you will actually *do*. For instance, "Improve SEO effectiveness" is a strategy but "Achieve 10 new high domain authority back links" is a tactic.

☞ Ideally your tactics need to have a mix of TTMs (Time To Markets) from today to multi-month. We can always add new tactics as our tactics get delivered...

Ó Don't make the mistake of picking too many tactics thinking that will make success somehow more likely. Every tactic added reduces the relative priority of all the other tactics so prioritise very carefully...

Đ "Fish!: A remarkable way to boost morale and improve results" by Stephen C. Lundin, Harry Paul and John Christensen. A fish market is studied to show how to bring energy, passion and a positive attitude to your job every day...available at https://amzn.to/2ZzOYG7

‡ A Capability Maturity Model Is a great lens to evaluate a team through...the levels most commonly recognised are...

Level 1 Initial - chaotic, ad hoc, individual heroics. The starting point for use of a new or undocumented software development life cycle.

Level 2 Repeatable - the SDLC is documented sufficiently such that repeating the same steps may be attempted.

Level 3 Defined - the SDLC is defined and managed as a standard business process.

Level 4 Managed - the SDLC is quantitatively measured in accordance with agreed-upon metrics.

Level 5 Optimising – Adaptive optimisation and improvement is in place.

Variable Capacity Talent

Everyone says that hiring the best talent possible is the most important thing...and they're right...but...you need a spectrum of talent in every team. Not all of a team's responsibilities are cool or ground breaking so a team consisting solely of high performers struggles to keep everyone equally challenged and motivated...

Ó Don't make the mistake of setting the hiring bar so high that very few people ever get hired. I have seen many teams struggle because nobody could ever match their unrealistically high hiring standards...

☞ Being flexible on office hours, working from home arrangements, office/remote locations and interim or permanent engagements may unlock the door to getting the talent you need to be successful.

I always look across three axes when hiring….1) Domain expertise 2) Impact focus and 3) Being a team player. Many hiring mistakes have been made by solely looking at domain expertise when hiring…

☛ We want the best talent possible but we need to take an optimistic approach. If you're 50:50 on someone then give them a chance. Probation periods are there to facilitate paperwork-light exits if a hire doesn't ultimately work out.

☦ At a business making redundancies after one of the financial crashes I saw less impact from one role compared with other roles but every time I suggested making this role redundant I got push back from the CEO saying that we couldn't make the person filling that role redundant as he was always the last person left in the office in the evening. It later transpired that the person was running his own Indian offshoring company from our office overnight!

Results v Relationship Focus

In general picking the right balance between being results and relationship focused at any point in time is hugely important. The need for both approaches will vary in time and across roles as well of course.

✝ The CFO at one of my interim engagements once accused me of being brought in to deliver the CEO's agenda "at all costs". He obviously felt that we were getting the Results v Relationship balance wrong so I made a conscious effort to make sure he felt that we were working with him (and not against him) much more going forwards...

Đ "INSPIRED: How to Create Tech Products Customers Love" by Marty Cagan is a master class in how to structure and staff a vibrant and successful product organisation. One of Marty's insights is that to create great products we should focus on misery, not on technology...great products fill great needs...available **at** https://amzn.to/2tZzJe5

« The most important thing about being a Tech Leader is that he/she should be well aware of their domain landscape and where the industry & technology needs to be steered towards. The leader should have good business acumen, be data & security oriented, be a people person and be a thought leader in his/her domain.

Sanjay Jadhav CEO LIFELabs

Ó A CEO once turned around to me as the CTO in April and said "I've told the board that we're setting up an offshore development operation in November so we need to do it". "Gulp" I was thinking before he finished off with "otherwise you're fired". Let's just say I thought he was getting the Results v Relationship balance wrong...

Đ "Steve Jobs" by Walter Isaacson is a brilliant look at what made Steve Jobs tick. As Steve Jobs said ..."The way we're running the company, the product design, the advertising, it all comes down to this: Let's make it simple. Really simple"...available at https://amzn.to/2F0vd16

Brilliant Basics

In any CTO ¦ CIO role there are usually core product ¦ service *delivery* responsibilities alongside the product ¦ service *development* responsibilities.

Ó Don't make the mistake of neglecting your product ¦ service *delivery* responsibilities in favour of your product ¦ service *development* responsibilities.

☞ There is nothing more important than delivering a great experience to your customers. You literally don't have a business without them. Your product ¦ service needs to be available, quick and easy to use at all times. If your app/website is unusable or down your shop is shut and shutting up shop is never a good thing for a business...

Ó Another mistake is to neglect the needs of your internal customer colleagues. Their tools and systems also need to be available, quick and easy to use at all times.

‡ In one interim CTO role I introduced an option for employees to use Apple laptops rather than the Windows standardised build laptops my predecessor had mandated. My colleagues were so over the moon with this change that they practically erected a statue of me in the car park. When you added up the cost of the corporate laptop, Microsoft Windows + Office software and docking station the Apple solution was actually cheaper overall as well.

☛ Getting your operational service delivery responsibilities right gets you your seat at the high table. Don't even think about trying to engage people in forward looking conversations if you're not delivering the best possible internal and external customer experiences *today*.

Small Teams

The founder of Amazon Jeff Bezos believes that no matter how large your company gets, individual teams should never be larger than can be fed with two pizzas.

‡ My team grew from 35 to 350 at Betfair and almost as academic exercise I used to try and analyse and model whether we were getting 10 X more delivery after a 10 X increase in overall team size. As we grew I got the feeling that we were hitting diminishing returns in terms of increased value of new hires and it looked like the teams were getting too big. I rearranged the structure into a set of smaller teams and it definitely improved velocity and overall delivery.

☛ A lot of the agile development approaches (stand-ups, scrum boards etc) assume sets of 8-10 person independent self organised teams.

☞ The number of relationships to be managed in a team of n grows as n^2 as n grows so there is a mathematical basis to the organisation theory hypothesis that a set of small collocated teams is the optimum way to organise a large group of people.

✝ One of my teams at Hailo was consistently underperforming and I was struggling to figure out why. They all seemed like great individuals, they were co-located and they seemed to be following the same sort of rituals as the high performing teams. Then one day it struck me...there was no diversity in the team of same age, same sex, same background people. I parachuted a different type of person into the team and the more diversified talent mix had a truly transformative effect on the team's delivery.

☞ Teams should include members with diverse backgrounds and approaches. You should do this not to tick any boxes but because it genuinely improves performance.

Problems Not Features

✝ Objectively measuring software development efficiency and effectiveness is so difficult because it is a design driven creative process. As much as 80% of the effort in good software production is in the design phase...and this is very difficult to analyse quantitively.

☞ Try to give your teams problems (such as improve X by Y%) rather than features to implement. As General Patton said "Never tell people how to do things. Tell them what to do, and they will surprise you with their ingenuity..."

Ó A team needs to be at the right maturity level before they should be asked to solve problems rather than deliver features. Doing this with an underperforming or immature team would be setting them and your company up for failure.

✝ We were suffering from low conversion rates at Betfair as people struggled to navigate the labyrinthine ten level deep menu structure to find the sporting event they wanted to bet on. One of the engineers had the idea of putting a search box on the front page (which was uncommon at the time). "OK" we said and happily watched revenue jump 30% on the day it was launched.

« The most wonderful thing about being a Tech Leader is helping to guide a team to grow its ability to take on ever more challenging projects... and watch their joy when they succeed on something they thought was near impossible.

John Eikenberry Director of Engineering

Đ "Accelerate: The Science of Lean Software and DevOps: Building and Scaling High Performing Technology Organizations" by Nicole Forsgren and Jez Humble is a detailed and clear discussion of best practice when it comes to building, deploying and running software...available at https://amzn.to/362CQzV

Professionalism

Business has become less formal over the years but there is no need for standards of professionalism to slide.

☞ Professionalism at work can be defined as behaving in a reliable, considerate, respectful and collaborative way in the workplace. Professional meeting behaviour might be to...

> Turn up on time.
> Arrive having done any actions assigned to you.
> Take notes using a laptop not paper (so you can easily reuse and search the text).
> Demonstrate your concern for the important issues facing the business.
> Proactively offer to help solve problems.
> Don't surprise or undermine any of the other people in the meeting.
> Stay present in the meeting, do not start using your phone, doing emails or whatever.

Ó Turning up late for a meeting is rude and inconsiderate. By turning up late for a meeting you are really saying to the people waiting for you that their time isn't as important as yours.

Ó One of the best ways of sabotaging your own success at work is by filling your calendar up with meetings. In most companies meetings aren't that productive so you're effectively making yourself unproductive. A self-imposed limit of 3-4 meetings a day should allow time for ad-hoc collaboration and working ON the team.

‡ My favourite joke about the importance of not being late is "I had a brilliant time at Fight Club last night...I was a bit stressed after turning up late and missing the beginning but Fight Club is a great white collar boxing club in the warehouse on Main Street..."

Culture

In reality a company culture is actually just the aggregate of everyone at the company's behaviours. You can't mandate a culture but you can influence it by role modelling and celebrating all of the positive behaviours you value.

Ó It only takes one person to poison a team culture...as Netflix founder Reed Hastings put it "Do not tolerate brilliant jerks. The cost to teamwork is too high."

Ð "The 7 Habits of Highly Effective People" by Stephen Covey has been a classic since 1989 and well worth a read. If you don't have time the habits are 1. Be Proactive 2. Begin with the End in Mind 3. Put First Things First 4. Think Win-Win 5. Seek First to Understand, Then to Be Understood 6. Synergise 7. Sharpen the Saw...available at https://amzn.to/2SvEki8

✝ I was working at one company when our web site crashed. The CTO came down to our end of the room and punched an open metal filing cabinet door...the noise reverberated across the open plan office like a car crash causing at least one member of the Tech Team to get up and leave...

≪ The most interesting/useful/important thing about being a Tech leader is being prepared for the unpreparable, you are only as good as the mistakes you make and how you fix them.
                    Leon Wynne, COO Amelco

☞ If there is mutual suspicion and sniping between two teams then mix them up and collocate them. I've done it at a number of companies and it normally resolves the "us and them" very quickly.

360° Communication

A modern workplace collaboration tool like Slack or Facebook Workplace really helps companies form a good collective identity, particularly if the teams are geographically distributed.

! Slack is a great way to maintain relationships with people in teams that a CTO ¦ CIO might not normally interact with very often such as Operations and Customer Services.

☞ Using something like Slack will reduce the number of meetings and emails you use to communicate and collaborate with your team and allow you to communicate in ways you hadn't had access to before.

Ó Don't neglect face-to-face leadership...line management activities such as weekly 30 minute 1:1s with direct reports, weekly leadership team meetings, quarterly all team meetings and annual appraisals are very important to your team members...

‡ At a recent interim gig I noticed in the Slack #customer-comms channel widespread unhappiness with what I thought was a minor bit of friction in the customer sign up process. I got the issue fixed and the customer facing teams were over the moon. It wasn't an issue they would ever have emailed the CTO about so I might not ever have heard about it without channel based communication.

‡ At Hailo Matt Heath integrated Slackbot with the Continuous Integration/Continuous Deployment pipeline so that code could be compiled, tested and deployed just by typing Build <Filename> in Slack.

Leader Of Leaders

We should all aspire to be a leader of leaders. Leadership behaviours should be role modelled and encouraged at all levels of the team.

! In 2008 Google launched an initiative called Project Oxygen to understand the behaviours that were common amongst their highest performing managers. Google think that the ten things that great leaders do are...

01. Coach their people
02. Empower their team and avoid micromanaging
03. Create a caring team environment
04. Be productive and results-oriented
05. Be a good communicator
06. Discuss development and performance
07. Have a clear vision/strategy for the team
08. Keep their technical skills up-to-date
09. Collaborate across the company
10. Be a strong decision maker

☛ Don't force great technologists to be poor people managers in order for them to achieve more status and reward. Create two ladders of equivalent roles and job titles in the Tech Team like this...

Technical Ladder	Leadership Ladder
CTO	CIO
Architect	Head Of
Senior Technologist	Manager
Technologist	Lead

‡ I'm told the most effective communication I ever do is a weekly email I like to send to my team called "Rorie's Ramblings". It has the same format every week including sections such as "One Thing I Did This Week", "One Thing I Learnt This Week", "What Made Me Laugh This Week" and so on.

Silver Bullets…

There are no silver bullets towards being a super successful CTO | CIO but if there were then maybe these would be our silver bullets…

USE A 🔫 MOST FRAMEWORK

CREATE 🔫 COMPETITIVE ADVANTAGE

BRING 🔫 URGENCY 🔫 CLARITY 🔫 DELIVERY

USE 🔫 AGILITY 🔫 SIMPLICITY 🔫 ACCOUNTABILITY

DEPLOY 🔫 GAME CHANGERS

That was a fairly brisk gallop through using a Mission Objectives Strategies Tactics framework to be a super successful CTO ¦ CIO but hopefully there was actionable insight on every page… please send any questions, comments or suggestions to **ctociobible@gro.team** … I'd love to know what you think…

« Read the CTO | CIO Bible, use a MOST framework, focus on business impact, don't neglect the basics, simplify wherever you can, employ agile approaches, encourage accountability and find your game changers...

Rorie Devine Interim CTO gro.team

☞ A free PDF version of this book (including updates and additions not publicly available yet) can be secured by apostles who help spread the word buying and publicly reviewing the CTO | CIO Bible ... to get hold of yours please email the link of your review to **ctociobible@gro.team**

Đ "Think, Do, Show: The Agile 2.0 Secrets to Building Software People Love to Use" by Simon Edwards is a brilliant guide to running high performance agile teams from a world class guy who really knows what he is talking about...available at https://amzn.to/2Q1R26D

A 01 CTO or CIO?

There is no right, wrong or universally accepted definition of what a CTO (Chief Technology Officer) is, what a CIO (Chief Information Officer) is, or what the difference between the two roles actually is.

Some companies have a CTO some companies have a CIO, and some even have a number of people with one or more of these job titles across their (usually large) organisation. What is generally agreed though is that both of these job titles entail running a "Technology"/"IT" Team as the most senior "IT" person in the business.

Ð "Elon Musk: Tesla, SpaceX, and the Quest for a Fantastic Future" by Ashlee Vance is an honest view of one of the most significant entrepreneurs of our time. Apparently, Elon had agreed to sell Tesla to Google before the employees came through on his request to sell three Tesla cars each...available at https://amzn.to/2tQwFk7.

Ð "The Hard Thing About Hard Things" by Ben Horowitz is an excellent reflection on Ben's experiences across a number of startups. The stand out quote is "If you're going to eat sh*t don't nibble"...available at https://amzn.to/2Mub8V1

Of course a company wants/needs both of the "CTO" ¦ "CIO" perspectives to varying degrees during different stages of its growth and it's why having *both* a CIO and CTO might be an optimum structure once a company has reached big scale or big complexity...

‡ I've done a number of jobs as both CTO and CIO trying to work the same way with both job titles. Everything worked out OK for me so maybe we shouldn't get too hung up on any perceived difference in the job titles...

A What is a CTO?

A Chief Technology Officer could be said to have a bias to working "IN" the team rather than "ON" the team.

SHe might have a bias to look "IN" rather than "OUT" from the IT/Tech Team. SHe should be passionate about existing and emerging technologies and how they can be used to create competitive advantage for their company. SHe might read Hacker News, Slashdot, have and use a GitHub account.

☞ A good CTO will have kept their core technical skills up-to-date. They won't have the time or experience to do every person's job in their team but they will have maintained a core set of technical skills that are up-to-date and relevant.

SHe might have come up through the more "technical" routes of Architect, Development Manager, Developer etc. SHe Is also normally the lead technology evangelist and advocate in the company.

« The most important tech things I've learnt as I grow older have come from the youngest and most inexperienced members of a team. Ignore them at your peril!

Richard Max Blockchain CTO nChain (bitcoinsv)

Đ Co-written by the captain of a US nuclear submarine "Turn The Ship Around!: A True Story of Building Leaders by Breaking the Rules" by L. David Marquet and Stephen R Covey is an excellent description of how empowering people can fundamentally change team performance...available at **https://amzn.to/353jk4Z**

A 03 What is A CIO?

A Chief Information Officer could be said to have a bias to working "ON" the team rather than "IN" the team.. SHe might have a bias to look "OUT" rather than "IN" from the IT/Tech Team. SHe should focus on getting a positive Return On Investment from the company's technology spend.

A CIO might dispassionately view the IT Team as just one of the teams in the company that needs to be cost effective and deliver the company's business plan. SHe might read forbes.com, wsj.com and is thinking about doing an MBA one day...

SHe might have come up through the less "technical" routes of Service Delivery, Programme Director, Project Manager etc. SHe very much views technology as a "HOW" not a "WHAT"...

A 04 What is Go?

Go/golang is an open source programming language created at Google in 2007 by Robert Griesemer, Rob Pike, and Ken Thompson. In computer language terms that very much makes it the new kid on the block (Java has been around since 1995 and PHP since 1994) but Robert, Rob and Ken have done a great job of bringing together all the best ideas from all the existing languages. As an open source project it is essentially free to use and Google say more than half of check-ins on the project are now done outside Google.

☞ We didn't have any golang developers at Hailo when we decided to move to it so our existing PHP and Java developers had to learn it "on the job". With a few exceptions they took to it like "a duck to water".

Golang is easier to write and manage than Java, it runs faster than almost everything except C/C++ and because it scales across multiple Cores/CPUs in a server "out of the box" you can save money by using less servers.

Faster

Go is a compiled language that compiles the source code programmers write down to the binary language servers can execute without further translation.

This is different to the interpreted languages like PHP/Python/Ruby that need to run on top of software interpreters. This makes Go significantly quicker in a straight line than scripting languages. (It's not even that much of a problem that you need to compile your code before you run it. The run command compiles and runs your go code so quickly that it's like working with a scripting language).

Go is so blisteringly fast that it is now actually being used to write a lot of the components underpinning the leading edge digital architectures. Docker (the rapidly growing virtualisation technology) is written in Go as is NSQ (the rock solid messaging platform) as is Bitly and so on...

Easier

Go is object based (rather than object orientated like Java) and has none of the fiddly memory management and pointer things you need to keep on top of in C++.

Because it compiles down to a binary executing Go code is as simple as deploying a file to a server and running it. There are no libraries, frameworks or interpreters to worry about.

Some people think the Go compiler is a little too fussy (it will complain if you include a library and don't use it for instance) but in combination with Go being a strongly typed language (I won't open that can of worms here) the upshot is that more errors are usually found at compile time rather than found at run time – and we'd much rather we saw any errors than our customers did.

Cheaper

☞ Go's killer feature is its concurrency model. Out of the box it will automatically create code that utilises multiple cores/CPUs by creating parallel executing threads. This is how companies like Hailo and Dropbox have achieved dramatic scalability improvements by moving to Go.

Ó With interpreted languages like Python, JavaScript, Ruby, PHP etc. even if they are technically multi-threaded only one thread can ever execute at one time (because of the Global Interpreter Lock).

‡ Hailo accidently found themselves as AWS's biggest customer in Europe by launching in more than 20 new cities by duplicating the London system and changing the city name to New York or whatever. We reduced the AWS bill by > 50% by re-platforming to Hailo 2.O which was a global Go based micro-services platform (see Boyan Dimitrov 's excellent SlideShare deck at http://bit.ly/hailoslideshare).

Any downsides?

There is no such thing as a "good" or "bad" computer language, they all have strengths and weaknesses, and you need to work back from the problem you're trying to solve before deciding which language is optimum for your particular circumstances.

☞ Go/golang is state of the art for use cases like backend APIs and micro services frameworks where you want low response times and low hosting bills, but it isn't really designed for the user interface layer...JavaScript is eating that particular world.

Golang's relative newness also means that there aren't as many libraries (chunks of code you can include and use) as existing for other languages. Good open source citizens like Dropbox are writing and open sourcing any missing ones as we speak.

There aren't as many golang programmers on the market yet as for other languages but we certainly found at Hailo that the opportunity to use golang attracted as many talented programmers as we needed and nearly all of our PHP and Java developers found it easy to learn and get productive on. Having two names (Go and golang) is a bit confusing and the Gopher logo is a little odd...but I'm nitpicking now.

In my experience a back end platform written in Go will probably be quicker, easier and cheaper than all the current alternatives but a lot really will depend on your business needs.

Not every business wants or needs minimised response times and maximised scalability and the cost of migrating an existing API/Platform is far from free of course.

A 05 Growth via Agile

By working closely and regularly with customers, delivering early, iterating ideas and working cross-functionally towards a common goal Agile software development transformed the business of creating software.

Agile development massively increased the value delivered by the typical software development project by favouring "individuals and interactions" over specification, "working software" over pretty much everything, "customer collaboration" over contract negotiations and "responding to change" over blindly following a plan...

What would happen if we used these "Agile" principles to deliver growth rather than Software?!? We could favour "customer collaboration" and "individuals and interactions" by forming a cross functional growth team including both "customers" and "suppliers". We should include representatives from Product, Sales, Marketing, Technology, Operations, Finance and so on...

We could favour "working software" or growth in our case by giving the team the single unifying purpose of growing a carefully chosen growth metric. The Growth Team could be "responding to change" rather than a plan by delivering early and taking a measure-act-measure approach to ideas through "on ramp" to "live" stages.

The Growth Team could communicate and meet regularly, maybe a quick "stand up" at the same time and place every day would work really well. We could work to a weekly or fortnightly rhythm with the cumulative effects of the growth activities on the Growth metric being publicly demonstrated (and hopefully celebrated) at the end of every cycle or "sprint".

So we have created a cross-functional team meeting regularly with the unified common purpose of doing anything and everything necessary to measure-act-measure the impact of their ideas on a single carefully chosen growth metric. That's cool but...Maybe we could give this sort of approach a name...like Growth Hacking or something?

Growth Hacking is the sort of term that means different things to different people but anyone familiar with Agile software development will be struck by the similarities between the approaches, rituals and rhythms typically used in both Growth Hacking and Agile Software Development. Does it all work in the real world? Yes.

☞ The same underlying principles that make Agile software development so effective also mean Growth Hacking can totally transform the effectiveness of a company's growth activities.

I spent a day with the talented team at a well backed UK based energy start up called Hometree who are creating a great brand by disrupting the domestic energy market customer experience. We had a really productive workshop where we honestly examined the Strength Weakness Opportunities and Threats in their current growth landscape, discussed and then selected initial and ultimate growth metrics, collected growth ideas, created a growth board, reconstituted the growth team and set up the new team's rituals and rhythms.

Not bad for one day and Andreu Tobella Brunet the Co-Founder of Hometree UK commented...

"As a start-up that is using an innovative way to sell online, we created a growth team from scratch but were having a few challenges to structure it well and have clear objectives and team alignment. This is where Rorie stepped in and helped us understand well all the roles, define our single metric and create a high performing growth team. The whole team was extremely pleased with the improvements, I would highly recommend him".

☛ Whether you call it Growth Hacking or something else, a very effective way of accelerating your growth is to learn from agile software development and to create a cross-functional team meeting regularly with the unified common purpose of doing anything and everything necessary to measure-act-measure the impact of their ideas on a single carefully chosen growth metric.

A 06 Success as an Interim

So what is the same and/or different about being an interim consultant vs full time employee, and how can you maximise your chances of success if you make the leap to being an Interim? In my experience very few people get treated any differently day-to-day in interim roles than "permanent" employees…the fact that you're an interim won't be a big issue but the expectations of you as an interim can sometimes be higher.

You might be expected to be an expert on more things, and you'll probably be expected to have a measurable impact – perhaps more quickly than a new full time employee would be.

☞ You could also get more latitude to challenge the orthodoxy, not be expected to navigate the company politics so carefully, and have your change agenda considered more dispassionately.

So how do you make sure you're successful in your first interim consultant role? The first (and maybe obvious) point is to choose the right role.

☞ Don't set yourself up for failure by taking an interim role with a team size, company culture or business model you're not absolutely confident you can add real value to. Ultimately what you "sell" is your reputation and track record – don't be tempted to risk it by taking on a role you're not 100% right for.

Once you have found the right role, and before you start, make sure you are very clear about the brief. Make sure you really understand what success will look like in the potential role. Sometimes companies want a change agent, but sometimes they just want someone to "act like they got the job for real" and do their "sensible best".

Make sure you understand whether you will need to be a good cultural fit or being counter-cultural is one of the reasons why they want to hire you. When you start get the basics right...always arrive on time and dress similarly to the prevailing dress code in the team.

At the early stages of any assignment make sure you don't write cheques you can't cash by promising unachievable things. There is no surer way of destroying your credibility (and making enemies of other people) than by promising things that can't be delivered. It's a subtle situation though...you may have been brought in to increase urgency and delivery so any goals you agree need to be ambitious but achievable.

☞ The most important thing to do when you arrive is to listen...never make the mistake of joining with a "here's the solution...now tell me about the problem" approach.

In your first week try and meet as many people in the team as possible. It's important for you to get to know the team, and them to get to know you, so scheduling 30 minute interviews with each team member to ask the sort of questions below will very quickly create a picture of what you're walking into.

Example interview questions…

01. Are you enjoying it here at the moment?

02. What are our key responsibilities as a team?

03. As a team, what do we do well do you think?

04. What do we need to get better at?

05. Who are our stars?

06. Does anyone need help to be more successful?

07. How could we get customer outcome focussed?

08. How could we move faster?

09. Would you recommend working here to a friend?

10. What three things would you do if you were me?

11. Anything else we should talk about?

After the interviews an interesting exercise is to allocate any team member mentioned as a "star" in Question 5 +1 and any struggling team member mentioned in Question 6 -1. Adding up all the scores will give a quick but surprisingly accurate team talent map. Question 9 can also be used create a quick team "NPS" score.

At gro.team we like to end the first week of a new assignment with a "Week One Playback" with the person that sponsored the appointment. It's a great opportunity to discuss the SWOT (Strengths, Weaknesses, Opportunities, Threats) found so far and calibrate it against what the sponsor wants.

☛ Remember to add value to your client in any way you can as well.

It's not just about the goals. Doing things like sharing their job postings on LinkedIn, mentioning them in any interviews you do, retweeting their tweets, liking their Facebook page, and so on, all help.

Don't "penny pinch" the client either. What "goes around comes around" so if taking a phone call or sending a quick email in non-client chargeable time helps solve a problem or keep momentum up then do it. You'll be judged on your impact at the end of the day.

👉 The last thing to remember is...to know when to move on. You know when you've achieved your goals or hit the diminishing returns point on the value curve. Don't wait to be replaced. Proactively suggest a new way to add value to the client if one is appropriate, or move on to your next challenge with another successful engagement under your belt.

So there you have it. To be a successful interim consultant you need to chose the right role, deliver as much value as you can, and then move on as soon as you've done it. We summarise it at gro.team with our motto of "Be Of Value". If you do that at all times you will be successful.

MEET THE AUTHOR

Rorie left his Managing Director job in Investment Banking to launch a self serve property market start up a few weeks before the biggest stock market crash since the war. When he ran out of money Rorie rejoined the world of paid employment as the CTO of a web design agency and since then has led more than twenty technology teams as both an interim and permanent technology leader/growth hacker.

Rorie is the only person to feature on the cover of CIO Magazine twice, has lead three of the fastest growing European startups ever and was awarded IT Leader of The Year by Computing magazine.

Rorie really enjoys working with clients as a Coach ¦ Mentor ¦ Interim and loves being part of the gro.team network of high impact interim consultants. Rorie also asserts that he invented (but never got the credit for) both Google Maps and fish finger sandwiches.

Ó If you didn't get the Fight Club joke then please remember Brad Pitt's speech to new members "The first rule of Fight Club is: you do not talk about Fight Club. The second rule of Fight Club is: you DO NOT talk about Fight Club!" Umm…I don't think comedy is my ticket outta here…

If you found this book interesting or useful please help get the word out with **http://bit.ly/CTOCIOBible** …

Made in the USA
Columbia, SC
21 February 2020

88222075R00049